Careers for

TECH GIRLS IN SOFTWARE ENGINEERING

SARAH ROSE DAHNKE

Rosen
YA™
New York

Published in 2019 by The Rosen Publishing Group, Inc.
29 East 21st Street, New York, NY 10010

Library of Congress Cataloging-in-Publication Data

Names: Dahnke, Sarah Rose, author.
Title: Careers for Tech Girls in Software Engineering / by Sarah Rose Dahnke.
Description: New York : Rosen Publishing, 2019. | Series: Tech Girls | Includes bibliographical references and index. | Audience: Grades 7–12.
Identifiers: LCCN 2017050836| ISBN 9781508180234 (library bound) | ISBN 9781508180241 (pbk.)
Subjects: LCSH: Software engineering—Vocational guidance—Juvenile literature. | Computer programming—Vocational guidance—Juvenile literature. | Women computer programmers—Juvenile literature.
Classification: LCC QA76.758 .D34 2019 | DDC 005.1023—dc23
LC record available at https://lccn.loc.gov/2017050836

Manufactured in the United States of America

CONTENTS

Introduction

Lola Priego grew up in Spain and thought she wanted to be a doctor. She hadn't even considered working as a software engineer because it was never presented as an option to her.

"For me, it was never a clear path at school," she says in an interview with the author. "I went to med school and never considered engineering because at my high school, none of the girls did engineering. [In college], the girl in the room next to mine was studying electrical engineering. We were studying in the library, and I saw she was doing all of these things with circuits and math, and I remember I was really interested. It was an eye-opening moment that this could be an option for me."

Priego changed majors from medicine to electrical engineering, and when a friend took her to a tech event, she met other programmers. This inspired her to teach herself how to code for Android, watching videos online and playing with sample code. Later on, she decided to formally study computer science and pursue a career as a software engineer. Now she works for Instagram.

According to the Bureau of Labor Statistics, employment in software engineering was projected to grow 24 percent between 2016 and 2026—much faster than the rate for most occupations—and it is on track to be one of the highest paying occupations. However, according to the National Center for Education Statistics, women earn only about 18 percent of

Women like Grace Hopper pioneered the "computer revolution." Most early computers were programmed by women, who also wrote many of the original software languages.

computer science degrees in the United States. There are so many exciting opportunities to apply software engineering skills in the tech industry, as well as in medicine, art, media, gaming, education, and more, and there is a real need for more women to occupy these roles.

In fact, women have contributed to software engineering throughout history. Ada Lovelace was considered the world's first computer programmer because, in the 1800s, she had the foresight to create an algorithm for a computer that hadn't even been built yet. During World War II, female mathematicians were hired by NASA as "human computers" to calculate ballistics trajectories because machine computers were not yet powerful enough to make the necessary calculations. In the 1950s, Grace Hopper created one of the first compilers to translate code to a language readable by a computer. The tech industry would not be where it is right now without the significant contributions of women.

Lola Priego encourages girls to experiment with code to challenge their brains and pique their interest, even if they aren't sure what career path they want to follow. "Coding is not super clear when you start," she says. "You don't exactly know how everything works. Just find resources and try different projects. I didn't wake up one day and say, 'Oh, I want to be a programmer.' I realized I was curious about this engineering thing, and I got into it."

Chapter one

WHY SOFTWARE ENGINEERING?

*S*oftware engineers are at work in almost every industry. Of course, we assume that, if we log in to our Facebook account or open our Instagram app, a team of software engineers helped create and maintain the product. But what about when you read the news on your phone, play a video game, have your medical records sent from one doctor to another, play music, or visit a museum? Software engineers are responsible for ensuring all of those experiences are implemented and run smoothly for all users. Because there are so many industry options, a software engineer's job could look very different depending on her expertise and field.

WHAT IS SOFTWARE ENGINEERING?

Software engineering involves designing, constructing, and testing applications by using computer programming languages. It involves creating, analyzing, and maintaining complex systems that meet the needs of the user. There are two main branches of software engineering.

Software engineers apply the principles of computer science, engineering, and mathematical analysis to the design, development, testing, and evaluation of software.

Applications software engineers create and maintain computer applications. This also includes mobile applications. Systems software engineers analyze technical needs department by department and create or maintain appropriate systems.

WHAT DOES A SOFTWARE ENGINEER DO?

The day-to-day work of a software engineer varies depending on her industry. Overall, software engineers are responsible for developing systems that allow computers to perform applications. With coding languages, software engineers can instruct a computer how to execute a function. However, while software engineers do need strong programming skills, their larger goals involve creating algorithms to solve more complex problems.

Computer programming is typically categorized as front end or back end.

FRONT-END DEVELOPERS

Front-end developers create the visible content on a website, web app, or mobile app and ensure the user can interact with it directly. Front-end developers want information to be structured in a way that is easy to use and is relevant to the product. They have to plan for variations in the way that a user may interact with a product, such as viewing it on various screen sizes, in different browsers, or on different mobile operating systems. Front-end coding languages are constantly evolving and changing, so a career in this field requires a dedication to learning and being aware of updates in the field. Front-end engineers often work with HTML, CSS, and JavaScript.

BACK-END DEVELOPERS

Back-end developers code the "brains" of an app, ensuring it can properly process user input. A developer who is programming in a back-end language interacts with the terminal, or console, in her developer environment to test and run code. This means she will see simple lines of letters and numbers, as opposed to the visual feedback a front-end developer may see. Back-end developers work with languages such as Ruby, Python, and PHP.

FULL-STACK DEVELOPERS

Full-stack developers can code across the full stack: front and back end. They offer the full package and can work with any of the languages utilized in front- or back-end development.

LEARNING COMPUTER SCIENCE

Your school may offer computer science classes, which you can take to get a feel for coding in different languages. If there are no computer science offerings at your school, you can still find a coding club, after-school program, weekend class, or summer intensive or participate in the wide array of free online programming. There are many initiatives that work to make sure young people have free access to computer science education even if they don't own a computer and have never written a line of code. If you're curious about coding, there is something out there for you!

SOFTWARE ENGINEERING LANGUAGES

There are many languages used in software engineering, and it is a field that is always developing and changing. However, there are some mainstays that are important for any beginning learner to become familiar with:

- **HTML:** Hypertext markup language is a language used for creating web pages and web apps. HTML describes the structure, or skeleton, of a web page and includes elements encased in tags that help a web browser translate visible content.

(continued on the next page)

There are numerous programming languages used in software engineering. Engineers must stay on top of current technologies and always be learning.

(continued from the previous page)

- **CSS:** Cascading Style Sheets works in tandem with HTML to provide style to the front end of a web page or web app. CSS makes a page visually interesting and engaging and helps to execute graphic and visual design.

- **JavaScript (or JS):** The majority of websites use JavaScript to execute dynamic visuals, and it is also used widely in video games. JavaScript is used to write web- and mobile-based apps and works with other languages to allow the display of animations and graphic-rich content.

- **Ruby:** Ruby is an object-oriented back-end language. It has been used to prototype apps that later grew into enterprises, such as Airbnb and Twitter.

- **PHP**: PHP is used in server-side (or back-end) development and uses scripts that can be embedded into HTML. It is commonly used to create desktop applications.

- **Python:** Similar to Ruby, Python is a widely used object-oriented back-end language. The creators of Python intended for it to be fun to use and named their language after the comedy show *Monty Python.*

- **Software frameworks:** There are a number of frameworks that act as a way to connect front- and back-end languages to fully form and deploy apps. Front- and back-end engineers are likely to utilize frameworks, some of which include Ruby on Rails, Sinatra, Django, CakePHP, and AngularJS.

IN SCHOOL

At the middle school level, computer science classes often utilize a drag-and-drop programming framework called Scratch, which allows students to play with and practice the fundamentals of computing concepts. Curriculum at the middle school level may also include basic robotics or physical computing with microcontrollers called Arduino, all of which operate on code customized and created on computers.

At the high school level, a CS class could take many forms. The most universal curriculum is AP Computer Science A, a course based in a language called Java, which utilizes many of the same principles and logic of other general purpose coding languages. High school courses may also offer robotics or mobile app development.

At any grade level, your school may have classes available for beginners with no experience, but also may require you to have made a certain grade in your math class as a prerequisite for computer science.

Not all schools have a computer science curriculum, but there are nationwide efforts to make CS available to all students. One of the organizations leading this effort is Code.org. It is a nonprofit dedicated to expanding access to computer science and increasing participation by women and underrepresented minorities. Code.org works to provide schools with resources to teach coding languages at schools around the world through its online curriculum.

AFTER SCHOOL

Even if your school doesn't offer a computer science class, it may partner with an outside organization to provide an after-school program or coding club. Google's CS First program is a free program for students in fourth to eighth grade. All curriculum is hosted online and led by teachers and community leaders. Google provides free materials for anyone

After-school programming classes and clubs are a great way to learn new skills and meet other people your age who are also interested in software engineering.

interested in leading a group, which could meet after school, on the weekends, or, in some cases, during the school day in a classroom.

Girls Who Code has a nationwide network of free coding clubs just for girls in sixth to twelfth grades. The clubs cover the basics of programming and lead participants in creating a group project. Clubs meet for two hours per week, either after school or on weekends. They take place in schools, libraries, and community centers and are led by facilitators, who could be volunteers from any background who are learning to code alongside the girls in the club. Girls Who Code also hosts a summer immersion program for girls in tenth and eleventh grade, where girls get experience at leading technology companies, such as Facebook or AT&T.

ONLINE

If you don't have access to a computer science curriculum at your school or through an after-school program, or if you want to supplement your learning, there are a number of free, web-based programs that will teach you any programming language under the sun. Online programs are usually self-paced and set up for learners at any level.

Google also facilitates an online program with a specific focus on girls called Made with Code. Girls can enter coding challenges and submit projects created with code, such as Snapchat geofilters, visualizing dance movements, engineering playlists and beats, and more.

Codecademy.com is one of the most robust online resources for learning programming languages. Students can take courses in specific languages or join an intensive with defined goals, such as building a website, an app, or an API. All code is written and tested inside of Codecademy's platform, so students can get immediate feedback.

SUMMER PROGRAMS

Why not get a leg up during the summer? Summer coding camps and immersions give girls an opportunity to focus on learning programming languages in a more intensive format, outside of the regular school schedule.

ENGINEERING APPS

O ne of the most obvious career paths for a software engineer is to land a job with a well-known tech company such as Facebook, Google, or Spotify. These companies need engineers to work on teams that deal with the mobile app development and web app development of their many products.

MOBILE APP VS. WEB APP: WHAT IS THE DIFFERENCE?

We typically think of an "app," or an application, as something we interact with on our smartphones, but in the context of software engineering, an application is anything created to take user input, process it, and give the user an output. Aside from our phones, we interact with apps on the web all the time, from typing search terms into Google to looking up new restaurants on Yelp. Software engineers are crucial to the creation and maintenance of both types of applications.

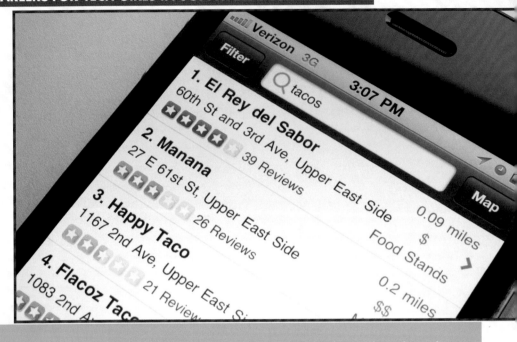

Engineers who create apps for mobile devices do a lot of testing on different phones and tablets to ensure the software works across multiple platforms.

Depending on the platform, software engineers write code in an integrated development environment (IDE) or a text editor for code.

MOBILE APPS

Mobile apps are engineered to run on a mobile device, such as a smartphone or a tablet, and they are either created to run on Apple's mobile operating system, iOS, or Google's mobile operating system, Android. Mobile app engineers typically specialize in one of the two platforms, although especially nimble engineers may become proficient in both or create cross-platform apps. iOS developers use an IDE called Xcode and write in Apple's mobile development language called Swift. Android development is open source, so there are many approaches to creating apps in this operating system. However, many Android developers work in Android Studio and code in languages such as Java, Kotlin, or C/C++. Both Apple and Google have free courses online that can teach beginners how to get started creating mobile apps.

WEB APPS

Web apps, since they run in the user's browser, can be created in a variety of ways in many different

Creating apps for desktop devices and the web also requires engineers to perform a considerable amount of testing for cross-browser compatibility.

programing languages. Web apps are typically engineered with a front end and a back end, which are then assembled via a software framework.

WOMEN WHO CODE

Women Who Code is a global nonprofit organization that envisions a world where women are proportionally represented as technical leaders, executives, founders, VCs, board members, and software engineers. The organization is comprised of women in tech, mostly engineers, with a dedication to keeping women in the field. According to the organization, women who are midway into their careers are leaving tech at a rate of 56 percent, which is more than double the quit rate of men. The organization attributes this to women having a much lower chance of being promoted, so it "focuses on changing the perception of the industry by highlighting the achievements and success of the diverse array of engineers that work in these professions."

According to Women Who Code, companies with a higher representation of women in leadership positions have seen a 34 percent higher return on investment than those with few or no women. Moreover, when women have higher incomes, they reinvest 90 percent of their income back into their families and communities. This creates "a virtuous cycle or multiplier effect for supporting women to earn more overall."

LOLA PRIEGO, SOFTWARE ENGINEER AT INSTAGRAM

For Lola, working at Google, Amazon, or Facebook was a big dream. She landed a job at Amazon after being rejected for a job for Google. "I was not really prepared. I didn't really know how much you have to study for these kind of interviews." Once she had a little experience under her belt, she was offered her current job at Instagram (which is part of Facebook), where she works with a team of other engineers to make Instagram run efficiently on low-bandwidth connections and offline.

"My projects have basically been Instagram offline mode and also Instagram background protection," she says. This allows you to consume this content even when you don't have cellular reception. "This project targets offline mode for emerging markets where people are very data-sensitive, or they may not have an Internet connection all the time. So we are trying to make it possible to use Instagram no matter where you are or what your data plan is."

Priego notes that her job is challenging and requires her to be at peak performance when she's at work. She says:

Every day I come and try to have new ideas. It's a creative job. On one hand, it's very difficult. You have the problem, and first you have to come up with a strategy that no one gives to you. The second part is implementation and experimentation and

Lola Priego loves the challenge that her job as an Android developer at Instagram provides. She discovered a love of computer science and engineering while she was in college.

proving that your ideas are moving in the right direction. Every day is a little bit different.

She has to make sure that she comes into work rested and ready to think creatively and logically for the betterment of her team. "I feel like I cannot come to work tired because I want my brain to be performing the best possible," she says. Luckily, at Facebook and Instagram, engineers are able to make their own schedules and work hours that suit their schedules and sleep patterns. "It's going to be better that I get more sleep and put in fewer hours because the hours I put in will be more productive," she says.

JOB OUTLOOK

Job outlook across the entire field is extremely promising. According to the United States Bureau of Labor Statistics, the field of software engineering as a whole was expected to grow 17 percent by the year 2024, which is a higher-than-average rate of growth. The same source states that web development was expected to grow 27 percent in the same amount of time. CNNMoney reported in 2017 that "mobile app developer" was one of the top one hundred careers in America, with job growth expected at a 19 percent rate by 2027.

Chapter three

ENGINEERING THE MEDIA

The way we consume news has changed dramatically. According to a 2016 report from the Pew Research Center, about four in ten Americans get their news online. Software engineers are now employed at every major media company, helping to push news to digital platforms on the web and through mobile apps. Every time you get a breaking news alert on your phone, a software engineer was behind creating the system that keeps us all up to date on what is happening in the world.

SOFTWARE ENGINEERING AND JOURNALISM

A career as a software engineer in news media allows for the creation and support of new, innovative ways of storytelling. Most newspapers have some type of digital presence on the web, and engineers work to create and maintain these online publishing platforms. Larger news organizations, such as the *New York Times*, the *Guardian*, and the *Washington*

Media companies employ software engineers and developers to deliver news updates to your phones and tablets as well as design unique mobile experiences for each publication's app.

Post, all create video content, some of which is in virtual reality or 360 degrees, and engineers are needed to build the structures that deliver the end products to users. Some of these organizations also find new ways to visualize and deliver data, all of which require the expertise of a software engineer.

JOB PREPARATION

There is room for all types of software engineers in news media, so women who are excited about engineering for mobile apps or the web will find a place. Make sure you are familiar with the product before an interview. Is it a large media company with several apps in different languages across the world? Is it a new company working to reach audiences in a unique way? At a larger company, an engineer's role may be very specific and devoted to just developing one facet of a website or mobile app, such as implementing digital subscription forms on each page. At a smaller company, an engineer may

Engineers with a passion for news are a commodity, as more and more people consume their news digitally. Some college majors focus on both computer programming and journalism.

wear more hats and work across web and mobile platforms, but she will be expected to have a wider breadth of knowledge.

Want to impress a potential employer? Have an app in your portfolio that speaks to your passion about news. You might experiment with pulling in breaking news or headlines about a specific topic from an application programming interface (API) that sends requests for news content. News organizations such as *USA Today* and the *Guardian* publish APIs, and social media companies such as Twitter provide ways to parse through data to just pull posts with certain keywords or hashtags.

KNIGHT LAB SCHOLARSHIP

Medill School of Journalism at Northwestern University has been offering scholarships since 2007 to software engineers who are interested in journalism. Awardees are given a full scholarship to the master's program in journalism followed by a six-month paid internship at the *Washington Post* on the software engineering team. Previous scholarship recipients have gone on to careers at companies such as Vox Media, National Public Radio, and the *Wall Street Journal.* While attending Northwestern, students also have a chance to work on projects in the Knight Lab, which develops software for journalists, publishers, and media consumers. It has a suite of projects that work with JavaScript that are used by digital content creators around the world.

CALLI HIGGINS, FRONT-END ENGINEER AT THE *NEW YORK TIMES*

Calli Higgins is a contract front-end engineer on the news products team at the *New York Times*, where she works on experimental products that enhance user experience on the newspaper's website—both desktop and mobile. She found herself in a job that excites her because she (a) loves to code and (b) is passionate about her company's mission. Higgins says in an interview with the author:

> This is a dire time for quality journalism, and the work that I do helps ensure we have that. Beyond that, the culture at the *NYT* is inclusive and supportive. I work with smart, respectful people in all stages of development. Our engineering team is focused on inclusive practices and we have a thriving Women in Tech group at the *Times*. Their accomplishments this past year alone include working with our CTO [Chief Technology Officer] to create a manifesto on Communications and Conduct, ensuring interview candidates are met with a gender-diverse interview panel, creating a robust new hiring process aimed at building a more diverse workforce, sponsoring tons of female hackathons, and so much more! Working for a company that prioritizes these efforts is very important to me and helps me do my best work.

Higgins also has a dream setup for many software engineers: she works full-time from home, communicating with her team via Slack and Google Hangout. "While I typically follow the same hours as my team, my unique working situation does give me the flexibility to write code when it is best for my brain, which for me is the afternoon into the evening," she says.

Higgins discovered her passion for coding as an adult, and she does not have a computer science degree. She says:

> There was a lot of catch up [to do] if I wanted to enter the workforce and collaborate alongside folks who did have engineering degrees. I used my work [from graduate school] to land a junior developer position, and from there I learned on the job. I have been fortunate to learn from a series of professional mentors

Calli Higgins now develops news products for the *New York Times* and previously worked as a developer for companies such as Estee Lauder and Samsung.

who, through extremely tough code reviews, have taught me both about best programming practices and how to work in a collaborative code environment."

Higgins also works as a computer programming instructor and has become a strong advocate for women entering the STEM field. She says:

There are so many small ways women can be discouraged from pursuing engineering. I'm frustrated that at no time along the path of my education did a teacher or advisor acknowledge my high math and science scores and encourage me to look into a STEM field as a career. It is a lot easier for a young woman to look at who society typically casts as a programmer, not see herself, and then assume she won't be good at it. Coding is not for everyone, but if you try it and it excites you, please know there is no shortage of engineering careers that will line up with your interests and hard work. You can love lipstick, video games, musical theater, or fashion (the list goes on forever) and be an amazing programmer who builds interactive experiences around those passions.

Chapter four

ENGINEERING MEDICINE

M ost medical devices require software to function, so there is a growing demand for software engineers within the medical field. Code is the backbone of everything from MRI and CT imaging devices, digital medical records and related security and privacy, medical education, and analyzing biomedical information.

WHERE ARE THE JOBS?

Software engineers can find themselves working at a hospital, a medical technology firm, a medical start-up, or as a research

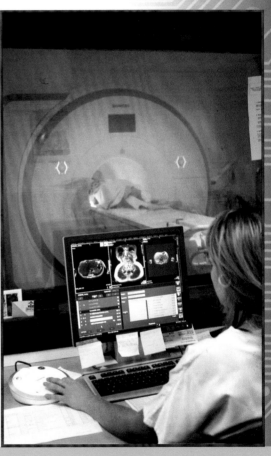

The medical technology field is booming, and software engineers are needed to develop devices and programs that help doctors better understand and diagnose patients.

engineer at a university, all contributing to important medical and biological innovations. There are also a number of apps that patients and health care providers use, which send reminders to patients or alert physicians about urgent medical needs. Most medical devices rely on some type of software to run, and this data is usually transmitted to a database. In all cases, software engineers are extremely necessary to ensuring the health of millions of patients and the research of lifesaving technologies.

MEDICAL TECHNOLOGY

Medical technology firms develop and test devices that are used by patients, physicians, or scientists. Software engineers are needed to create user interfaces, process data, mine data, build databases, and more. An engineer may find herself working on new devices, but it is more likely she will be iterating on and improving preexisting medical technology to make it more efficient, cost effective, and safer to use.

MEDICAL START-UPS

Start-ups in the medical field are likely to be pursuing the implementation of new technologies, which can be an exciting place to find yourself working. Engineers may be working in the same capacity as at a more established medical firm, but the technologies may not yet be on the market. Start-ups will likely be engaged in clinical trials and FDA approval to bring their products to the public.

RESEARCH ENGINEER

Research engineers work on teams, often at universities or other research institutions, to design and investigate new medical technologies and devices. Software engineers could find themselves working on cutting-edge technologies to test and operate medical devices that are innovative and recently conceived, such as assistive technologies for individuals with the loss of limbs, eyesight, hearing, memory, and more.

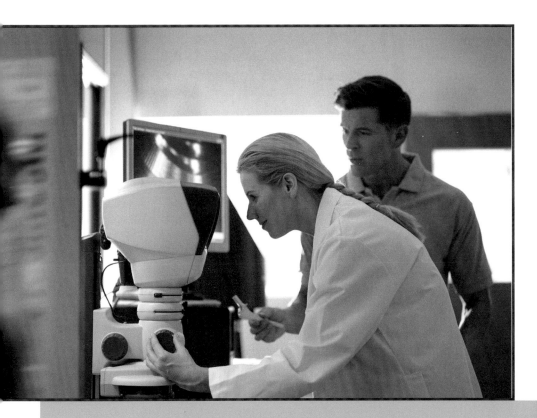

Some software engineers work for companies that focus on research, writing and maintaining programs to process data, or help power medical devices that are not yet on the market.

JOB PREPARATION

Medical technology is a rapidly changing field. If you have a passion for the integration of medicine and software engineering, your best bet is to articulate *why.* Are you excited about contributing to software that could help cure certain diseases? Are you committed to working in an organization with a focused mission? Do you have an interest in medicine? A software engineer at a medical company is not expected to understand medicine the same way a doctor might, but it is helpful if she has an interest in contributing to the field. Job growth in the field is very promising, too. According to the Bureau of Labor Statistics, employment of engineers in biomedicine was expected to grow 27 percent by the year 2022. Software engineers will be a large part of that employment growth.

BIOINFORMATICS

If you have a passion for biology, data, and computer science, you may consider a career related to software engineering: bioinformatics. This field of science focuses on analyzing DNA to better understand genetic bases of diseases. Bioinformatics scientists sequence DNA, store them in databases, and use programming languages to analyze, search, and compare genes. There is also an ongoing need for developers to create new tools and algorithms to analyze data. There is a large open-source movement within the bioinformatics field, with a focus on creating free, open software in the life sciences. This movement is led by the Open Bioinformatics Foundation, which supports the Bioinformatics Open Source Conference. Those interested in bioinformatics may consider an online certification, available for free through platforms such as Coursera's Bioinformatics Specialization through University of California, San Diego; Genomic Data Science Specialization through Johns Hopkins; and edX's Data Analysis for Life Sciences XSeries through Harvard.

Love DNA and data? Bioinformatics is a growing field that is expected to increase in growth by 8 to 10 percent between 2014 and 2024.

ANASUYA DAS, SENIOR DATA SCIENTIST AT MEMORIAL SLOAN KETTERING CANCER TREATMENT CENTER

Anasuya Das is a senior data scientist at Memorial Sloan Kettering Cancer Treatment Center (MSK) in New York City. Her job is to work collaboratively with other data scientists and engineers to write code and use machine learning to solve problems. "Our team is a cross-disciplinary team that leverages software engineering, data science, and design to build software that can be used by care providers to ultimately treat cancer better," she says in an interview with the author. She also meets with doctors and other care providers to better understand their needs, which influences the products they are building.

"I really appreciate being in a mission-driven institution and working on problems that have a major impact on people's lives. I also like that the team is really collaborative and cross-disciplinary and that I can work so closely with such a diverse group of people," Das says. Working as an engineer in a cancer treatment facility is also an incredible challenge. "Anytime we build something it's both risky and difficult, so we have to be very, very sure that what we build is accurate, reliable, and can be trusted by doctors," she says.

Das has a personal connection to the work she is doing, which inspired her to apply her technology-based skills in the medical field. Das says:

Someone very close to me is a cancer survivor. It made me realize just how much complexity and uncertainty there is in both providing and receiving healthcare. I'd like to believe that tech and data science can to some extent help with the problems that are faced by doctors and patients, and that brought me to MSK. She advises girls considering a tech-based career in the medical field to go for it. She says:

Tech is inherently collaborative, and technology by definition is a human endeavor that needs people like you to build it. If you are excited by the future, by new ideas, and [you] like to create and build things, consider tech. But also consider tech if you like working with people and want to have an impact on people's lives. Don't be afraid to learn and try things. Don't be afraid to take apart things no matter who built or created them. Ask questions about everything!

Chapter five

ENGINEERING ENTREPRENEURSHIP

Maybe you will create an app one day that has the ability to fill a niche that no one else has yet filled, or you will find a more creative and efficient solution to a problem. You could pitch your app to funders and get enough money to hire a team! Many software engineers learn to code as a way to build projects that they want to bring into the world.

BRINGING AN APP IDEA TO LIFE

Even if you don't have venture capitalists throwing millions of dollars at you, you can still prototype your idea and get feedback from mentors and peers. Prototyping is the act of creating a model of a product so that it can be tested by users before you expend valuable development time on creating the actual product. It lets people "play" with your app, so they can see what it does and give you advice about moving forward. Even beginners can engineer a solid idea, conduct some user testing, and eventually release an app online or in a mobile app store for the masses to use.

Many entrepreneurs debut their apps on the Apple App Store. Apps that have large numbers of downloads are often highlighted on the front page, increasing visibility.

JOB PREPARATION

The fun thing about being an entrepreneur is that you don't have to interview with anyone to land a job. You are your own boss! That being said, some practice with prototyping app ideas will definitely help you prepare for when you have that million-dollar idea. Keep a notebook full of app ideas that you'd like to see in the world, and create some wireframe mock-ups of what they may visually look like. Pick one of your favorite ideas and see if you can create a minimum viable product (in the tech world, referred to as an MVP), to demonstrate what your app would do and how it would work. Define your audience. Who is this app for? Does your app solve a problem that needs to be solved or find a new take on a solution? Apps that are created for a niche that has not yet been filled are usually the ones that have the potential to take off.

WOMEN WHO TECH START-UP CHALLENGE

The annual Women Who Tech start-up challenge has provided seed funding for startups led by women that create digital tablets for the blind, engineer 3D printed artificial limbs, redistribute unused medicine, and make smart, wearable emergency safety devices. Since 2015, the organization has awarded more than $1 million in prizes, crowdfunded dollars, and investments.

Women Who Tech was founded "to bring together talented and renowned women breaking new ground in technology to transform the world and inspire change." The Women Start-up Challenge, in particular, was founded because, according to the organization, "a whopping 90 percent of investor money worldwide goes to startups founded by men." That number has barely changed since the mid-2000s. "We know that there are many women start-ups that have the right ideas, whose products can solve problems, and can change the world. But to scale and be successful, these start-ups need funding, advice, and guidance."

Start-up challenges are a great way for teams who have developed a prototype of an app to reach potential investors and get funding to develop it.

KRISTINA BUDELIS, FOUNDER OF KITSPLIT

Kristina Budelis used to be a freelance video producer and found she was spending too much time and money picking up camera and production gear for shoots. She knew there must be a better, more streamlined way to engineer this process, and as a result, she created Kitsplit. Kitsplit is an online platform that allows individuals to rent out their camera and video production equipment in a marketplace that has been described as the "Airbnb for cameras." She is now the founder and president of the company, and she was on the 2017 *Forbes* 30 Under 30 list, celebrating her innovation.

While she was in graduate school, Budelis created a quick prototype of Kitsplit using a template and doing some minor adjustments to the HTML and CSS. This allowed the idea to gain some press and get Kitsplit into an accelerator program, which provided the first round of investment to the idea. She says in an interview with the author:

Along with a small development and design team [we] built a new version of the site from scratch. I'm so glad we started on the pre-built platform, though. This really helped us learn what worked and what didn't before spending a ton of time and money we weren't confident about!

Have an app idea? Find the fastest route to a prototype, so that you can show your innovative ideas to people who can provide guidance, support, and funding.

Now that Kitsplit is a full-grown company with growth in multiple cities, Budelis's role is constantly changing. She says:

The nature of working at a small start-up is that you're constantly learning new things and taking on new challenges. One thing that's changed over time is that our team has grown, so more of my time is spent supporting my teammates and making sure they have the right tools to succeed. I'm passionate about the product we're building and the community we're serving, and I'm humbled by the awesome team I get to work alongside every day.

She has two pieces of advice for girls who may want to create their own app or eventually lead a start-up company:

1. "Find a cofounder—or if not a cofounder, a close adviser or mentor—who is excited about the idea and can be a sounding board. There are so many tough decisions and tough moments when you start a business that it's important to have a support system to get advice from, or just vent to!"

2. "Start small. I think sometimes people have no idea and get overwhelmed by how difficult it would be to build. Ask yourself: 'What's the very simplest version of what I'm trying to make?' And do that first. Just get something out there, and get feedback."

Chapter six

ENGINEERING VIDEO GAMES

These days video games exist everywhere, from game systems to web-based games to apps on smartphones, and there is a need for adventurous software engineers to help create new games as well as maintain and improve long-standing

The video game market for PCs and mobile devices is expected to continue to grow, earning $132 billion in revenue by 2021, according to a report by Juniper Research.

games. The video game industry employs thousands of software engineers, many of whom have also studied or have experience in the field of game design. However, the gender gap in the video game industry is huge.

According to an article in the *Boston Globe*, women accounted for only 11 percent of game designers and 3 percent of programmers in 2013, compared with the broader fields of graphic design and technology, where women make up about 60 percent and 25 percent, respectively. The *Globe* also notes that the overall percentage of women employed by video game companies is increasing, but nearly all that growth is in nontechnical fields such as public relations.

Despite female underrepresentation at video game companies, women still play video games just as much as men. In fact, the number of women playing video games increased by 70 percent in 2014, while the number of male players only increased by 43 percent, according to the Entertainment Software Association. And while the stereotypical idea of a gamer is a nerdy teenage boy, in reality adult women represent 31 percent of video game players, while teenage boys make up only 18 percent. With so many women playing video games, there's a real need for more women to be engineering them.

ON THE JOB

Video game software engineers can work on a variety of tasks that that contribute to creating video games.

INTERNATIONAL GAME DEVELOPERS ASSOCIATION WOMEN IN GAMES SPECIAL INTEREST GROUP

The IGDA Women in Games Special Interest Group was formed to create a positive impact on the game industry with respect to gender balance in the workplace and the marketplace. The IGDA WIGSIG offers community, resources, and opportunities to those looking to break into the business. The group creates a supportive, positive atmosphere for women in games and communicates networking opportunities to its members through a very active mailing list and social media presence. The WIGSIG also maintains a speaker bureau, which is a collection of diverse speakers for game development and tech events. Members can nominate themselves or colleagues to be included, thereby opening up who is publicly represented in the industry.

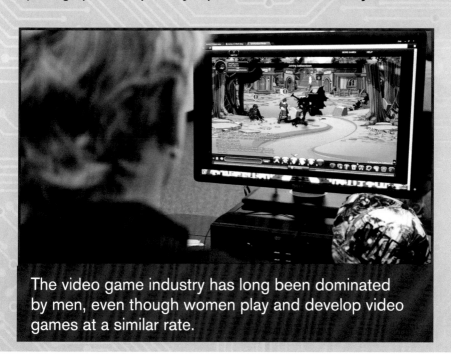

The video game industry has long been dominated by men, even though women play and develop video games at a similar rate.

They create software to help games run and also engineer the animations that create characters, game worlds, and more. Artificial intelligence is used often in games, and engineers are responsible for creating the algorithms behind it. Some game engineers are more involved with the design of the game and how characters interact or how users will interact with the game.

JOB PREPARATION

A software engineer who is interested in a career with a video game company may want to look into additional studies in game design. Game design curriculum includes two-dimensional and three-dimensional animation, information management, artificial intelligence, and lots of practical experience making and testing games. This, coupled with the knowledge of some programming languages, will make anyone a very attractive candidate in the video game field.

Additionally, you could practice designing simple games in different languages to keep your skills sharp. A common two-player game like tic-tac-toe could be coded in basically any programming language and in configurations such as human versus human, human versus computer, and computer versus computer. Software engineering from a game perspective relies heavily on a concept called object-oriented programming, which is a powerful model that organizes around actions and objects, rather than data and actions. Becoming familiar with object-

The video game industry is no longer a "man's world." There is a need for more games to be developed with a woman's perspective in mind.

oriented programming will be necessary in even the most introductory software engineering positions in the video game world.

AMY JO KIM, PROFESSOR AND CEO OF SHUFFLE BRAIN

Amy Jo Kim is a woman who has found her way in the male-dominated video game industry for quite some time. She is a professor of game design at the University of Southern California's Cinematic Arts program and the CEO of the game company Shuffle

WOMEN'S RIGHTS IN THE WORKPLACE

Women are often the victims of various types of discrimination in the workplace, and it is important to go into a professional environment armed with knowledge of your rights. The American Civil Liberties Union defends women's rights in the workplace and works to ensure that all women—especially those facing intersecting forms of discrimination—have equal access to employment free from gender discrimination and wages equal to their male counterparts. Pregnancy discrimination has been illegal for decades but still sometimes occurs in the workplace, with women losing employment, wages, or promotions as a result.

If you are ever sexually harassed in the workplace, take notes on the harassment and report it to a supervisor or human resources department immediately. If harassment persists, you can file a complaint with the Equal Employment Opportunity Commission, which is responsible for enforcing federal laws that make it illegal to discriminate against a job applicant or an employee because of the person's race, color, religion, sex (including pregnancy, gender identity, and sexual orientation), national origin, age (forty or older), disability, or genetic information. It is also illegal to discriminate against someone for complaining about discrimination, filing a charge of discrimination, or participating in an employment discrimination investigation or lawsuit.

Brain. She has worked as a game designer on games such as *Rock Band* and *The Sims* and contributed to the design of the interfaces of eBay, Netflix, Lumosity, Happify, and more.

In 2006, drawing upon her experience in the game world and her PhD studies in neuroscience, she authored the book *Community Building on the Web: Secret Strategies for Successful Online Communities*, which uses the concept of game design within the context of how successful brands build communities of people who regularly return. The book was groundbreaking and launched Kim as a pioneering thought leader and the first to bridge the concepts of game design and digital services. The book has become wildly successful in the game design field and remains required reading in many university programs.

Kim has been named by *Fortune* magazine as one of the top ten influential women in games and is a sought-after keynote speaker.

Chapter seven

ENGINEERING ARTS

M any artists use code to reflect on the world around us, make political statements, or imagine different futures. There are artists who use coding languages as another tool, like a paintbrush or camera. Technology can be used as a canvas for creativity and innovation, taking in data and processing it in an interesting, aesthetically pleasing, confrontational, or unique way. The thing that unites art projects made with code is that they all are built with a basic understanding of how computers think. Whether it's a piece of fabric designed by visualizing election data or graphics generated from an algorithm that analyzes sound, principles of software engineering can be applied in the most rule-bending of ways.

LIFE AS A MEDIA ARTIST

Creative coding is another way a software engineer may use her skills, displaying her work online, in galleries and museums, or in unexpected places. Many digital artists work with software engineering and code, but they may also integrate other technologies, such as cameras, drones, circuits, and more traditional art techniques such as painting, sculpture, or photography. Many digital artists have

Some artists use creative coding to create projects that utilize intricate data visualizations and camera tracking or to program hardware that is integrated into their artwork.

found success through similar pathways as traditional artists, gaining representation by galleries and selling their artwork to collectors.

JOB PREPARATION

Life as an artist who uses software engineering could look much different from the previously mentioned careers. Art may be your main focus, or "artist" may be one of many hats you wear as a software engineer. If you are visually inclined, experimenting

Camera or motion tracking uses algorithms to tell a camera to follow motion. Artists sometimes use this technology to create installations that create interactive visuals.

with data visualizations is a great way to play around with making something beautiful from code. Data visualization describes any effort to help people understand the significance of data by placing it in a visual context. Patterns, trends, and correlations that might go undetected in text-based data can be exposed, recognized more easily, and presented in unexpected ways through the process of data visualization. There are many amazing women doing creative work in this field, including Camille Utterback's public installations, Fernanda Viégas's poetic visualizations, and Lauren McCarthy's digital interrogations of social interaction (as well as her work creating p5, the JavaScript sketchbook).

SPOTLIGHT ON RHIZOME

In conjunction with the New Museum in New York City, nonprofit arts organization Rhizome commissions, exhibits, preserves, and creates critical discussion around art engaged with digital culture. The site acts as a digital gallery of tech-based artworks and commissions browser-based creations. Outside of the digital space, Rhizome curates exhibitions of creative technology in the New Museum's galleries. Through its flagship program called Seven on Seven, Rhizome pairs artists and technologists to create together and unveil the results at major public events. Because of its commitment to preserving digital art, Rhizome created a digital preservation program that allows for public access to Rhizome ArtBase, a collection of more than two thousand digital-born artworks. It is also responsible for the creation of free and open-source software tools that allow for the continued growth of the digital art field.

HEATHER DEWEY-HAGBORG, ARTIST

Heather Dewey-Hagborg is an artist who works with science and technology, experimenting with algorithms and human DNA in her practice. "I use art as a way of thinking through and with science and technology, understanding it and its impact on society in a material and experimental way," she says in an interview with the author. In her body of work, Dewey-Hagborg has created several pieces that comment on human surveillance and privacy. In her piece *Stranger Visions*, she collected remnants of human DNA through items such as chewed up gum found in New York City. She extracted DNA from these items and analyzed it to computationally generate 3D-printed life-size, full-color portraits representing what those individuals might look like, based on genomic research.

Dewey-Hagborg says:

Science and technology are political and are huge influences on culture. Art allows us to explore and understand these fields differently. Sometimes that means it exposes problematics of the fields, the potential for biological surveillance for example, but at other times art can harness potentials of these fields for liberatory purposes.

As a college student, Dewey-Hagborg found herself interested in art, new media, and computer science, and the crossover of all of these fields eventually led her down the artist career path she finds herself on today. She says:

Programming led me to artificial life and an ongoing fascination with conceptions of the "natural" and "artificial." Engaging with machine learning algorithms led me to thinking about biology and biodiversity and evolution as these were the processes computer scientists were trying to model through genetic algorithms, neural networks, and cellular automata.

Dewey-Hagborg is grateful that her interdisciplinary studies eventually led to a career that she loves. She says:

Heather Dewey-Hagborg is interested in art as research and critical practice. She has shown work internationally at venues including the Centre Pompidou and MoMA PS1.

I feel so incredibly lucky that I get to spend my time pursuing projects of my own imagination and not having anyone else telling me what to do. The best thing about being an artist, I think, is that it is such a vastly open field. You can do anything.

And for any girls thinking of bringing their interests in art and technology together to follow in her footsteps, she is here to encourage you to do so. She says:

I think the most important thing is to dream big and learn widely. Art and technology is at the intersection of entire networks of different fields of study. Read everything you can get your hands on—philosophy, social science, humanities, current events—and experiment in a hands on way with new technologies. Get into a hacker space if you can, and try making things from scratch. Write code. Culture some bacteria. Think about how everything intersects. Don't listen to anyone who tells you your ideas are silly or impossible. Just about everything you can dream up is possible with the right conditions.

Chapter eight

ENGINEER YOURSELF!

O nce you have some skills under your belt, the best way to continue on the path to a software engineering career is to get some real-world experience. It's one thing to learn coding languages, but another to actually apply them to creating solutions for companies or clients.

BUILDING YOUR PORTFOLIO

To land that first gig, be it a job or an internship, you will increase your chances with some evidence of experience on your résumé. Employers may be interested in which programming languages you've learned and how long you have been studying, but they will also want to see some code you have written and projects you have engineered. These can be projects you created in a class or on the side for fun. They do not have to be professional projects yet! It is expected that beginning learners will have created most of their code in some type of learning atmosphere.

GITHUB

Lots of programmers, developers, and software engineers use GitHub to publish their code and share it with others. It's a simple way to show people what you are working on and get inspired by the work

It's never too early to create an account on Github and start pushing code. Github is a great way to interact with other developers of all experience levels across the globe.

of others. Potential employers will likely want to see a link to your GitHub profile, so they can get a sense of your style of coding and projects you have created or contributed to. Familiarity with GitHub will also be an attractive quality to a potential employer because it will demonstrate you know some aspects of version control, a system used by most software engineers that records changes to a file or set of files over time.

BLOGS

Another awesome way to demonstrate your skills and reinforce your learning is to publish a blog that can walk readers through your thought process when coding or creating. If you attend a coding boot camp, a blog is often a requirement for graduation, as it shows that you can walk through a detailed process and teach it to a reader. A blog doesn't have to be fancy; you can set one up for free on Tumblr, Medium, or another platform of your choice. Already have a website? That's a great place to showcase completed work, and you could add a blog to your growing online portfolio.

TECHNICAL INTERVIEWS

If you land an interview for a job or internship in a technical role, be prepared to answer some questions about programming languages you know and your education, and give a technical breakdown of any projects you have made. You may be asked to go more in depth about your process or even to build some sample code on the spot. Don't be intimidated by this process! Any good interviewer will also provide you with some feedback that will help with your next technical interview.

FLEXING YOUR SKILLS: HACKATHONS AND TEACHING

Even if you're just beginning your learning journey, there are so many ways to get out there, meet other cool girls who are coding, and collaborate.

Hackathons are events at which computer programmers and others involved in software engineering collaborate intensely over a short amount of time to create usable software.

Hackathons are a great way to just dive into building something with code—sometimes with people you've never met. And there are lots of opportunities to reinforce your skills through teaching and assisting with beginning coding classes as you move through your software engineering education.

ALL-FEMALE HACKATHONS

Hackathons typically last at least twenty-four hours, if not a few days, and bring together a large number of people to collaboratively program projects. They are sometimes organized around a theme, and there are a few hackathons that are specifically for women and/or people under the age of eighteen.

WiCHacks is an all-women's twenty-four-hour hackathon hosted by Women in Computing at Rochester Institute of Technology. Hackathon participants can be female college or high school students who are at least sixteen years of age. It is open to women of all skill levels, including those who have never written any code before. WiCHacks even has a Newbie Track, which teaches basic programming skills alongside the hackathon. All teams are formed at the kickoff, so participants don't have to arrive knowing who they will be working with. Previous winners of the hackathon have included an app-based robot that helps you fix coding errors in a game setting and an app that looks like a food delivery app but allows domestic abuse victims to contact the police.

TEACHING THE NEXT GENERATION OF TECH GIRLS

In addition to developing your own career in software engineering, you may want to spend some of your summer break, after-school hours, or weekend helping other girls learn to code. You could start a coding club and learn a new language along with some of your peers. Or you could apply to be a teaching assistant with a more advanced coding boot camp, working side by side with more experienced teachers and software engineers and reinforcing what you have learned.

Carson Levine has been a teaching assistant for Introduction to Software Engineering with Upperline School of Code since 2016. She started coding

Teaching is a great way to reinforce your skills and act as a mentor to other young women who also have an interest in programming.

during the summer after her sophomore year of high school, when she had the opportunity to take a couple of two-week immersive courses in software engineering. "Until then, I never understood what programming exactly was, and I had an itching to find out," she says in an interview with the author. Ever since she scratched the itch, she has continued to create things with code. She used her web development skills to create an online magazine called *TeenEd*, subsequently called *The ISH* (the-ish. co), and gathered a group of fifteen friends to write content and help develop it.

Working as a teaching assistant has been an rewarding experience for Levine. She says:

> It's been incredible helping high schoolers understand powerful concepts that I am so passionate about. It's remarkable to watch people transform as they begin to realize their own capabilities. I learn so much from each classroom about coding, teaching, and people, and have appreciated working with such a variety of inspiring individuals.

As a computer science student herself, she is still very hungry to keep learning. "I can't wait to learn even more code, gain new skills, and create new things!" And for the future software engineers of the world, she has just one piece of advice: "If you're ever debating whether or not to pursue something, just go for it!"

Glossary

ALGORITHM A process or set of rules to be followed in calculations or other problem-solving operations, especially by a computer.

APPLICATION (app) A specialized program, created for mobile devices or the web, that takes in user input, processes it, and gives back an output.

APPLICATION PROGRAMMING INTERFACE (API) Provides developers with standard commands for performing common operations so they do not have to write the code from scratch.

ARTIFICIAL INTELLIGENCE Development of computer systems able to perform tasks that normally require human intelligence.

COMPUTER SCIENCE The study of computing, programming, and computation in correspondence with computer systems.

ENGINEERING The design and manufacture of complex products.

INTEGRATED DEVELOPMENT ENVIRONMENT (IDE) A software application that provides comprehensive facilities to computer programmers for software development.

MINIMUM VIABLE PRODUCT (MVP) A development technique in which a new product or website is developed with sufficient features to satisfy early adopters.

OPENSOURCE Software for which the original source

code is made freely available and may be redistributed and modified.

PROTOTYPE A first, typical, or preliminary model of something from which other forms are developed or copied.

SLACK A platform commonly used by technical and creative teams to communicate and share files and code snippets.

STEM Science, technology, engineering, and math, all of which are becoming more strongly implemented in K–12 education.

TEXT EDITOR In reference to software engineering, this is an application or piece of software where code is written and tested.

VENTURE CAPITALIST An investor who either provides capital to start-up ventures or supports small companies that wish to expand.

VIRTUAL REALITY Computer-generated simulation of a three-dimensional image or environment that can be interacted with in a seemingly real or physical way by a person using special electronic equipment, such as a helmet with a screen inside or gloves fitted with sensors.

WIREFRAME An image or set of images that displays the functional elements of a website or page, typically used for planning a site's structure and functionality.

For More Information

Anita Borg Institute's Annual Grace Hopper Celebration
Website: https://ghc.anitab.org
Facebook: @anitaborginstitute
Twitter: @AnitaB_org
The world's largest gathering of women technologists. It is produced by AnitaB.org and occurs in a different city each year.

Built by Girls
Website: https://www.builtbygirls.com
Facebook, Twitter, and Instagram: @BuiltByGirls
Organization committed to making sure girls have access to futures in tech. Program offerings include a pitch competition, a regular speaker series, and an immersive internship that showcases what it takes to be a start-up founder and investor.

Code.org
Website: https://code.org
Facebook: @code.org
Twitter and Instagram: @codeorg
A nonprofit dedicated to expanding access to computer science and increasing participation by women and underrepresented minorities. Reaches students through a variety of web-based curriculum tools.

Codecademy
49 West 27th Street
New York, NY 10001
Website: https://www.codecademy.com
Facebook, Twitter, and Instagram: @codecademy
Web-based programming curriculum in many
    languages. Curriculum is self-paced and gauged
    for all levels of learners.

Geek Girl
3539 Curtis Street
San Diego, CA 92106
Website: http://geekgirlcamp.com
Facebook, Twitter, and Instagram: @GeekGirlCamp
Organization with a mission to create a more
    diverse workforce in tech, build tech bonds
    between children and their parents, and help
    girls become their own tech superheros. Geek
    Girl hosts full-day tech conferences, workshops,
    seminars, and consulting.

Girls Who Code
28 West 23rd Street, Floor 4
New York, NY 10010
Website: https://girlswhocode.com
Facebook, Twitter, and Instagram: @GirlsWhoCode
Organization committed to building the largest
    pipeline of female engineers in the United States.
    Girls Who Code facilitates coding clubs and
    summer immersive programs.

Google CS First
Website: https://csfirst.withgoogle.com/en/home
A free program that increases student access and
    exposure to computer science (CS) education
    through after-school, in-school, and summer
    programs. All clubs are run by teachers and/or
    community volunteers.

International Game Developers Women in Games
Special Interest Group
19 Mantua Road
Mt. Royal, NJ 08061
Website: http://women.igda.org
Facebook: @IGDAWomen
Twitter: @IGDA_WIGSIG
Group formed to create a positive impact on the
    game industry with respect to gender balance
    in the workplace and the marketplace. The
    IGDA WIGSIG offers community, resources, and
    opportunities to women and men in the games
    industry, as well as those seeking to break into
    the business.

Kode With Klossy
Website: https://www.kodewithklossy.com
Facebook, Instagram, and Twitter:
@KodeWithKlossy
Empowers girls to learn to code and become
    leaders in tech. Hosts girls' coding summer
    camps, awards career scholarships to young

women developers, and helps create a national community changing the role of girls and women in tech.

Made with Code
Website: https://www.madewithcode.com
Facebook and Instagram: @MadeWithCode
Fun, creative, online coding projects with a focus on girls, created by Google with a mission to make sure women are represented in the technology industry.

Upperline School of Code
New York, NY, and Greenwich, CT
Website: https://www.upperlinecode.com
Facebook: @UpperlineCode
Immersive summer and weekend programs teaching back-end and front-end web development to high school students. Focused on teamwork and collaboration in the learning process.

WiCHacks
Rochester Institute of Technology
1 Lomb Memorial Drive
Rochester, NY 14623
Website: https://wichacks.io
Facebook: @wic.hacks.rit
Twitter: @wichacks
An all-women, twenty-four-hour hackathon hosted by Women in Computing at Rochester Institute

of Technology. Participants create an app, website, game, or other piece of software over the course of the event.

Women Who Tech
Website: https://www.womenwhotech.com
Twitter: @WomenWhoTech
A nonprofit organization founded to bring together talented and renowned women breaking new ground in technology to transform the world and inspire change. Hosts the annual Women Start-up Challenge around the world.

For Further Reading

Alston, Sasha Ariel. *Sasha Savvy Loves to Code.* Plano, TX: Gold Fern Press, 2017.

Briggs, Jason R. *Python for Kids: A Playful Introduction to Programming.* San Francisco, CA: No Starch Press, 2012.

Gonzales, Andrea and Sophie Houser. *Girl Code: Gaming, Going Viral, and Getting It Done.* New York, NY: HarperCollins, 2017.

Marji, Majed. *Learn to Program with Scratch: A Visual Introduction to Programming with Art, Science, Math and Games.* San Francisco, CA: No Starch Press, 2014.

Martin, Chris. *Build Your Own Web Site* (Quick Expert's Guide). New York, NY: Rosen Publishing, 2014.

Niver, Heather Moore. *Getting to Know Ruby* (Code Power). New York, NY: Rosen Publishing, 2014.

Niver, Heather Moore. *Women and Networking: Leveraging the Sisterhood.* New York, NY: Rosen Publishing, 2012.

Strom, Chris. *3D Game Programming for Kids: Create Interactive Worlds with JavaScript (Pragmatic Programmers).* Raleigh, NC: Pragmatic Bookshelf, 2013.

Suen, Anastasia. *Internship & Volunteer Opportunities for People Who Love All Things Digital (A Foot in the Door).* New York, NY: Rosen Publishing, 2012.

Sweigart, Al. *Automate the Boring Stuff with Python: Practical Programming for Total Beginners.* San Francisco, CA: No Starch Press, 2015.

Bibliography

Android. "Developers." Retrieved September 17, 2017. https://developer.android.com/index.html.

Apple. "Start Developing iOS Apps (Swift)." Retrieved September 17, 2017. https://developer.apple.com/library/content /referencelibrary/GettingStarted /DevelopiOSAppsSwift.

Boyer, Justin. "History of Women in Software Engineering." *Simple Programmer*, September 18, 2017. https://simpleprogrammer .com/2017/09/18/female-software-engineers.

Bridge, Faye. "What Types of Developers Are There?" Treehouse, June 24, 2016. http://blog .teamtreehouse.com/what-types-of-developer -are-there.

Burrows, Leah. "Women Remain Outsiders in Video Game Industry." *Boston Globe*, January 27, 2017. https://www .bostonglobe.com/business/2013/01/27 /women-remain-outsiders-video-game -industry/275JKqy3rFylT7TxgPmO3K/story.html.

Byrne, Ciara. "The Loneliness of the Female Coder." *Fast Company*, September 11, 2013. https:// www.fastcompany.com/3008216/the-loneliness -of-the-female-coder.

Chang, Angie. "12 Great Pieces of Advice from Female Software Engineers." Hackbright Academy, December 29, 2014. https:// hackbrightacademy.com/blog/12-pieces-advice -female-software-engineers.

Computer Science Degree Hub. "Is There a
    Role in the Healthcare Industry for Computer
    Programmers?" Retrieved October 1, 2017.
    http://www.computersciencedegreehub
    .com/faq/role-healthcare-industry-computer
    -programmers.
Doyle, Alison. "Top Technical Interview Questions."
    The Balance, July 7, 2017. https://www
    .thebalance.com/top-technical-interview
    -questions-2061227.
Gaudiosi, John. "10 Powerful Women in Video
    Games." *Fortune*, September 23, 2014. http://
    fortune.com/2014/09/23/10-powerful-women
    -video-games.
GitHub. "Crowdsourced Repository of Women
    in Software Engineering Stats." Retrieved
    September 14, 2017. https://github.com
    /triketora/women-in-software-eng.
Interview with Anasuya Das, Memorial Sloan
    Kettering. New York, NY. September 28, 2017.
Interview with Calli Higgins, *New York Times*. New
    York, NY. September 25, 2017.
Interview with Carson Levine, Upperline School of
    Code. New York, NY. October 6, 2017.
Interview with Heather Dewey-Hagborg, Dewey-
    Hagborg Studio. New York, NY. October 10, 2017.
Interview with Kristina Budelis, Kitsplit. New York,
    NY. September 26, 2017.
Interview with Lola Priego, Facebook/Instagram.
    New York, NY. September 18, 2017.

Kozlowski, Lori. "Women in Tech: Female Developers By the Numbers." *Forbes*, March 22, 2012. https://www.forbes.com/sites /lorikozlowski/2012/03/22/women-in-tech-female -developers-by-the-numbers/#77a8d5641760.

Luscombe, N. M., D. Greenbaum, and M. Gerstein. "What Is Bioinformatics? A Proposed Definition and Overview of the Field." National Center for Biotechnology Information. Retrieved October 17, 2017. https://www.ncbi.nlm.nih.gov /pubmed/11552348.

Murthy, Sohan. "Women in Software Engineering: The Sobering Stats." LinkedIn, March 20, 2014. https://business.linkedin.com/talent-solutions /blog/2014/03/women-in-engineering-the -sobering-stats.

Percival, Alaina. "10 Reasons Why More Women Should Work in Software Engineering." *Wall Street Journal*, August 5, 2014. https://blogs.wsj .com/accelerators/2014/08/05/alaina-percival -10-reasons-why-more-women-should-work-in -software-engineering.

Sahadi, Jeanne. "Now Hiring: Women with These Degrees." CNNMoney, July 7, 2016. http://money .cnn.com/2016/07/07/pf/women-engineering -computer-science-degrees/index.html.

Index

ABOUT THE AUTHOR

Sarah Rose Dahnke is a graduate of the creative technology master's program at ITP/NYU and studied full-stack web development at the Flatiron School in New York. She's an instructor of media arts and teaches web development to beginning learners, with a focus on educating girls. Dahnke is a former professional dancer who still creates and teaches choreography when she's not coding.

PHOTO CREDITS

Cover Syda Productions/Shutterstock.com; cover, interior pages (circuit board illustration) © iStockphoto.com/Vladgrin; p. 5 Bettmann/Getty Images; pp. 8, 26, 62 Hero Images /Getty Images; p. 11 iinspiration/Shutterstock.com; p. 14 Kansas City Star/Tribune News Service/Getty Images; p. 18 Bloomberg/Getty Images; p. 19 David Lees/Iconica /Getty Images; p. 22 Courtesy of Lola Priego; p. 25 chainarong06/Shutterstock.com; p. 29 Courtesy of Calli Higgins; p. 31 BSIP/Universal Images Group/Getty Images; p. 33 Monty Rakusen/Cultura/Getty Images; p. 35 4X-image/ E+/Getty Images; p. 39 Bloomicon/Shutterstock.com; p. 41 Yuri_Arcurs/DigitalVision/Getty Images; p. 43 Joos Mind/The Image Bank/Getty Images; p. 45 Wachiwit/Shutterstock.com; p. 47 ZUMA Press Inc/Alamy Stock Photo; p. 49 Photo by Casey Rodgers/Invision for Microsoft/AP Images; p. 53 Andor Bujidoso/Alamy Stock Photo; p. 54 ukartpics/Alamy Stock Photo; p. 57 Courtesy of Heather Dewey-Hagborg; p. 60 Casimiro PT/Shutterstock.com; p. 64 Westend61/Getty Images.

Design and Layout: Nicole Russo-Duca; Editor: Rachel Aimee; Photo Researcher: Karen Huang